somewhere else

poems by

MATTHEW SHENODA

COFFEE HOUSE PRESS

Minneapolis

COPYRIGHT © 2005 Matthew Shenoda
COVER & BOOK DESIGN Linda S. Koutsky
AUTHOR PHOTOGRAPH © Madame Athena Chang

Coffee House Press books are available to the trade through our primary distributor, Consortium Book Sales & Distribution, 1045 Westgate Drive, Saint Paul, MN 55114. For personal orders, catalogs, or other information, write to: Coffee House Press, 27 North Fourth Street, Suite 400, Minneapolis, MN 55401.

Coffee House Press is a nonprofit literary publishing house. Support from private foundations, corporate giving programs, government programs, and generous individuals help make the publication of our books possible. We gratefully acknowledge their support in detail in the back of this book.

LIBRARY OF CONGRESS CATALOGING-IN-PUBLICATION DATA
Somewhere else : poems / by Matthew Shenoda.
p. cm.
ISBN 13: 978-1-56689-173-8 (alk. paper)
ISBN 10: 1-56689-173-6 (alk. paper)
1. Egyptian Americans—Poetry. 2. Coptic Church—Poetry.
3. Egypt—Poetry. I. Title.
PS3619.H4538S66 2005
811'.6—DC22
2004027803

5 7 9 8 6
Printed in the United States

For my parents & ancestors
who gave me lineage.

All my teachers living & ever-living.

For all of the Coptic people
& roots-life peoples around the world.

Contents

Living Ancient

Paying homage is about the acceptance of an inheritance, the refusal to forsake ancestors, community, class.

—MARTÍN ESPADA

I do not seek education, I seek inspiration. If I was educated I'd be a damn fool.

—BOB MARLEY

There got to be a message within the music, so the knowledge of the children will increase.

—ISRAEL VIBRATIONS, "Rebel For Real"

I know time, time is gonna take its toll. We are gonna have to pay, we've got to pay for the love that we stole. It's a sin and we know it's wrong.

—ARETHA FRANKLIN, "Dark End Of The Street"

ZULU PROVERB:

*"A word uttered
cannot be taken
back"*

and so I say:

Freedom!

Introduction

In this country, where history stretches in aristocratic silence, a young poet has come at the beginning of the 21st century, carrying the quiet urgency of a star. And the country is not the same.

I say, who is this poet who sings down the lids of deserts with color?

I say, I say, who is this poet always punctual with his eyes, his heart, his hands?

I say, I say, I say, who is this poet who mixes poetry and philosophy, who leads us into, "the skulls of the ancients" residing in the Eastern Sahara: "Each sphere of bone / a voice // A cage / of warrior mind."

What does "Coptic" taste like? Is the Nile the color of Tātās? Is nature sentimental? Forgetful? Does it have a long memory? As Matthew Shenoda begins to answer these questions, as he resurrects summer language on our winter landscapes, as he anoints our eyes with ancestral light, we see the spine of the Nile, the sand of old flesh, the tapestry of language like sequins on our eyes. We are immortality among the Relics: "I am the once-severed arm of a young girl / scrambling for a foothold in this desert . . . I am the fingers of a woman whose knuckles live beneath the flower box // We remember each other through these bones."

José Martí wrote: "In the world there must be certain degrees of honor just as there must be certain degrees of light. When there are many men without honor, there are always others who bear in themselves the honor of many men. . . ."

I turn the corner of this honor-driven book, find memory beneath our doors, taste the blessings of his midwifery, his miracle songs giving birth to un-ghosted rooms, his poems coming to us glittering like silver stars, and I catch them in mid-flight, swallow them whole.

Behold the poet, questioning the flesh of national conventions: "where color means a beating / if your taillight flashes / anything other / than English."

Behold the poet, speaking about our children: "how many years must our children watch / the building of caskets, the withering of leaves / by graveside, by tombstone, by the rotting corpses / of their peers . . . I am living in the rifle adorned with stickers from sixteen-year-old soldiers who pretend that this life is normal // our trees are fed by the blood of our sisters / our fruit is sour, our soil is rich / our children wail shards of glass / our youth wear guns for shoes . . ."

Behold the poet: shaking dew from the drums. . . .

Behold the poet: calling for rebellions, "rebellion like the hand reaching for what it cannot hold / the child whose dignity is greater than her beating / to survive beyond the soil / to see beyond your self / believing only one . . ."

Tolstoy said, not that an artist should write about the masses, but that he should be intelligible to the masses and Matthew Shenoda's poems are convocations of shimmering truths sequestered on our feet. Hands. Eyes. Blood.

Behold the poet!

—Sonia Sanchez

Transparent Ancestry

New Cairo

The furniture still smells the same.
The street echoes
voices of peddlers,
the marketplace.
The basket hangs off the railing
they use it to pull up corn, bought
from a passerby.

I stand on the balcony, staring
withdrawn from this poverty by a mere generation
then I remember:

Great-Grandmother used to say,
"If you throw salt away
God will make you
pick it up
one grain at a time
with your eyelashes"

Lineage

Our people
carved the coffins
and etched them with arcane script
laid the shrouds
by way of tradition
and through the grace of Thoth
began to record our history
embalming after embalming
antiquity was preserved
sealed
like a rock before a tomb.

Thoth was the Egyptian moon god said to be
the inventor of spoken and written language.

Remembering

The mason came
from Pharaoh's garden
preparing to erect a tomb,
calling upon grace
he cleansed his hands
and whispered:

From this place
I will shape
the memories of inevitable generations
&
in this place will they be remembered.

The Nile Before Being Dammed

This is the story of my people,
the story of us all.
Banks lined with reeds and papyrus ready to be scrolled
water tables gifting us the crops of this season.

The scent of my people builds in my hands as I work
nets of sustenance;
untangling, realigning,
singing:

Pull up sail on the felucca
We've just one river to cross
The reeds that line her banks
Will write us all back home
Swinging palms and fresh, ripe dates
My life is on that shore

Oh sweet bearer of wind
carry my felucca to the river edge
bless me with a line of fish
and let the great hippo swim one more day.
The rising of waters has given us bread
drink and fortified life
olive and lime
mint and mango.

The arid fields of tomorrow
give strength for one more time
separate the flax from the husk
hook the oxen to the mill and grind
dear friend, grind
your labor feeds us all.

Yesterday's Tar, Tomorrow's Pavement

The elders tell of a man,
whereupon invading his small delta town,
the enemy stripped him of his clothes
and dipped his nude body in tar.

They captured a poor creature
—a buffalo—and with her tail, tied the man to her haunches,
beat her and watched
the abused parade the town square.

The people came from their homes.

From balcony tops the ruling class cheered.

But the elders hid and prayed:

The children
The children
God teach the children

In the night the elders broke from their homes
to collect the body.
Bloodied and tarred
they dressed him in his sanctified garb
and left him in the center of town
scorched and unburied for all the children to see.

What we have seen, forever let it be
What we are.

Prayer

The sun sets over monasticism
two thousand years of chants and prayers
seclude themselves in the eastern desert.

Many among us will pray for rain
for rising of waters
plentiful crops.

Some will pray for answers
revelations on papyrus scrolls.

I ask only for peace
for open skies and land to walk,
the rest will find itself.

Homeland Poem

Having been
dealt poverty
we cannot afford to buy
the lies they're selling

Song of Name

Inside the illuminated song
floats a note
that only the ancient can hear
three scales above the rest
it rides through the ear
deep past the bone
driven by the engines of memory
the ancient transforms
to living
and the song of Name rings clear
sounding:

Agios

Sounding the Meander

I am the troubadour of sound

a walking drum in rain

I am a saxophone come live

the sound of sugarcane

I am the plucking of a bass

the revelry of style

I am the music of the living

I am the River Nile

Song of Re-Call

For every verse sung
a bone is collected
from among antiquities   victims
one by one they are reassembled
graciously and in accord
they begin to move

to move

to move

to dance

A Prayer for My People

That one day
we will wish
to be nothing more
than what we are.

That we will see
within ourselves
the liberation of nations, of concrete.

That we will understand
the inevitability
in the lines of our hands.

There is a war raging in our backyard
With it my sister's spirit burns

That the fire of my sister's spirit
will consume our enemies
& burn our streets clean.

There's a system of mangled necks
Whose heads speak with oracle tongues

That we should learn to walk
with wounded feet

That our eyes must be liberated
from their granite

That our hands re-root themselves
from the pools of acid rain

> There's a river forming in the bureaucrat's head
> Its water made from rusted milk

That we may understand this false constructed world
& know:

Holy things
Do not die!

Somewhere in the Eastern Sahara
There Is a Wall Made of Skulls

Down from the shadow of Mount Sinai
a couple days from the Red Sea,
lost in the barren
space between
there is a place
where monks carved
culture's rock.

Like the hands of the sculptor
dusty with imagination
each sway of their arms
shapes the desert.

We woke one day
under the ancient Saharan sun.

We made our way to the inner desert
to the quiet place.

Summoned and asked to witness
what has never been seen before.

We began digging rock
for a wall sixteen centuries old
we found the skulls
of the ancients.

Each sphere of bone
a voice

A cage
of warrior mind.

Hammering nails with rocks
constructing pine boxes
each skull was set
in the wall's interior
to watch those who approach
by night.

Where eyes once shifted for fear
a stiff-straight gaze appeared.

The way one human being
can forgive another
in that moment
where shadows ascend
and vanish
somewhere in that silent understanding
we lend ourselves to one another
knowing survival would be impossible
without it.

Tātās

Our grandmothers walked the banks of the River Nile
Balancing on their heads alabaster jars.

Our *tātās* beat clothing on the banks of the River Nile
Ringing and rolling the precious drops against limestone rock.

They dried the dates of palm on the banks of the River Nile
Adding to their sweetness a kiss of peace.

They carried the weight of the River Nile
The weight of us all, on their backs, all the while bracing earth with
    their toughened feet.

Tātā is the colloquial Egyptian word for "grandmother."

Red Sea

Our sea is a beautiful sea
one that distracts us from poverty & barrenness
she sings to us in green
rises to touch us
like the bare hands of a lover
her currents erode our memories of pain
finger us like domical spheres
smoothing the inner collapse of our chests
into well-worn ruts
so that each of our beloveds
can lay their heads beside us
and hear her sing smoothly.

Aswân

Between the thumb and the index
There is understanding
To be guided by a rudder
Is the job of the felucca
Not the human being.

He submits to prayer on the bow of the boat
Bending with the Nile's current
It matters little in that moment
Where he is
Only that the will to give is in him.

Laughter emerges like a cracked tooth
Sheltering the tongue from the grit of the earth.

Every child blessed with hands, works
Understanding that survival mixes well
With the playful spirits of imagination
Learning early that black tea
Sedates the rage of the most fearful.

Provisions arrive only with struggle
The poor learn never to beg
Only to release themselves to the waters
Pull up sail and be carried by wind.

Blue

Traveling to the song of calamity
the heart is a wrinkled mast
the soul as formed as the bow.

The songs we sing
when sorrow
has taken flight in us
these are the songs we remember.

Annunciate

Annunciating the struggle
knees sunk deep
on the banks of the Nile
on fire
hippopotamus beats and papyrus realities

remember how they skinned our brothers thin

sewed the flesh of the dead to our tongues

gifting us the evaporating taste of stealth

the language of another brother's skin

Annunciate
like the campesinos cultivate

Annunciate
in the tradition of your people's fate

Annunciation
breaks silence & starvation

Keep it real

ṣaḥīḥ
ṣaḥīḥ

with that hectic eclectic
Cairo-style Copticism

Ṣaḥīḥ is the Arabic world for "real."

Relics

Scrabbling bones together like a gathering of river stones

Bones become sacred
Human remains, memories of cartilage
Piled centuries high
Skulls and leg remnants begin to tell the stories of before.

I am the once-severed arm of a young girl
Scrambling for a foothold in this desert
Where once my enemy chaser did not live

I am the fingers of a woman whose knuckles live beneath a
    flower box

We remember each other through these bones
Through the songs of calcium deficiency and famine strings that
    strum us into night
We are the gathering of old-timers whose eye sockets tell stories
    of victory

We are a memory shaped by vertebrae
Clappers of rhythm disassembled by the skeletons of time

I am the kneecap of a man whose only hope was grounding toil
Scrubbing my skin with the earth for food

I am the elbow of children whose eyes twitched at the thought
of cold

I am the shin of garbage collectors building stamina for a city
to come

We are a memory shaped by vertebrae
Clappers of rhythm disassembled by the skeletons of time

We are the dissipating cartilage of our great-grandchildren's
memory holding to their sockets by a sinew of hope

Making sense of these bones we reassemble history
Making ancestral tapestries in the shape of retaining walls

We are a memory shaped by vertebrae
Clappers of rhythm disassembled by the skeletons of time

You are the skin behind the clouds

The Calendar We Live

As it was, it is
and so shall it be
from generation
to generation
& unto the age
of all ages. Amen.
—COPTIC PRAYER

It is 1717 AM

Time   a question
only the Nile can answer
meandering through papyrus fields & *baqara* expanse
her sediment the testament of Coptic

Out in the eastern Sahara monks drink chocolate milk in the
          "cantina" celebrating Epip's big feast.
It is hot   olive trees grow like tiny worlds of sweat
          magnified on foreheads
planted here by a memory sixteen centuries old

Incense lifts from sand in unison with chants

Gazelles roam cliffs at orange dusk, eating fish-bone trash &
     smirking at the stars strung around their necks

We have two homes, two histories
out here in Sahara, right there on the Nile

One thousand seven-hundred & seventeen years since
     Diocletian tried to erase us

One thousand seven-hundred & seventeen years of
     remembering what civilization could be

years of a nonviolent branded brown fist
     bare knuckle to the concrete prostrating

integrated memories and
     tattooed wrists swirling in the solace of community

a tradition that rises from
     blood

Too many years After Martyrdom

through this struggle in the funk of oppression & constant fight
we give our children love
their faces inquisitive with rise-up brows
feet strong & planted
they walk the banks of

rippled erosions
burrowing through
Nile Valley terrain
meandering like octopus
swinging tentacles through space

we take the walk beside them
with hopes they will not sail to the other side

      displaced in a place we call home-now
1969 was our exodus
fleeing the land of other
the diaspora of promise
wearing the sandals of broken english

& what do I become
in this world where rivers and deserts collide
the deep red sea of generational memories
swishing & spitting pacific images
in this forever-west

bridging the gap of *ṭabla* & hip-hop
citrus & hibiscus
I hit the streets of Cairo
kicking up dust
like airbrushed worlds of flat ghosts
eyes blinded by the butcher's hanging carcass

suspended by metal like a condor wing
punctured by a gnarled branch
somewhere beyond this place

I imagine streets as a village
viable & crop-rich
flowing with silk humanity
eyes fill the alleys
black corneas float in an expanse of muslin
ṭabla rhythms & *shīsha* smoke
creep from corners

I am somewhere between
home & home

trying to see ourselves
moving through rivers of translation
transported relics
mixed with spices & myrrh
preserved ancestor tongue
stiffer than bone
fluid like leaves when autumn's song is audible
when skyscrapers make way to
desert breakers
& long bearded nomads
remain still in Sinai caves
while white tunic spirits roam the lands that surround them

the sphinx upon a rock
I am
son of civilization
daughter of flat bread

made fresh on the bellies of coal
speaking fire, *pi-ekrom*
fire branding memories
until *pi-ekrom* becomes
an-nār, becomes fire
fire on the tongues of memory
mo-ou our skin
water our shelter

and then   the lexicon
covered in gold, in it
a truth, a single truth, whose only name is
History

and on the day that lexicon is opened to Coptic
it will read:

bury me in the skin of my mother
the mask of my father
understand that we are
one breath
living for that single moment
where voices congregate
pitching into the unknown

pitching a song the enemy cannot hear

so we sing to our children
in their moments of terror
carrying olive branches in their left hands
struck by batons and wicked words

you are the viable one
whose story has not been stolen
whose roots dig deep
in delta waters

1717 AM: One thousand seven-hundred and seventeen years After Martyrdom
   on the Coptic Calendar
Baqara: Arabic; Cow
Epip: Coptic; a month that coincides with parts of June and July on the
   Western calendar
Ṭabla: Arabic; traditional Egyptian drum
Shīsha: Arabic; hookah, used to smoke flavored tobacco
Pi-Ekrom: Coptic; the fire
An-Nār: Arabic; the fire
Mo-ou: Coptic; water
The Olive branch in the left hand is a symbol from ancient Egyptian art. The
   olive branch representing peace; the left hand, the side of the heart.

30

Living Ancient

Somewhere Else

It is here on this ridge
exposed to the orange dusk
of mountain autumn
that the story begins.

Buck wood for the stove
feel the heat of shoulder to tendon
greet the mule deer
and water the garden again.

In rhythm, with song
when the ax begins to blend with wind
carry on to warmer days
on the river's open banks
where the fervor of healing is found in water.
Flow from one origin to another—
there is never a place where we cannot begin
where the current is ancient, the wind is young
teaching each other like the ax and the wood.

Carve a place for dignity
plant a seed and pray for rain
for sun
for understanding outside your self.

There will come a day when they say:
who do you think you are
and another day will come
for you to tell.

On that day the story will appear
but do not tell of yourself

tell the story of the staff that blossomed in the desert
or the one about your enemy's greatest victory

tell the story of somewhere else.

Transporting a Weed Whacker
Way Over County Lines

for Anthony

Many months back
my grandmother came home
to Egypt
saw my uncle, her son
boasted to him of America's
simple yet efficient invention
the weed whacker.
He smiled in interest.

It is now the future
my brother and I entering
Egypt with a gas-powered
weed whacker
in a golf bag
as if we were going to play
eighteen holes on the Sahara.
We laugh at expected remarks
from the customs man
instead, he yells *yallā*
go ahead
we break free into
Cairo's crowds.

Standing on the Corner

Waiting for a cab on Cairo's streets
scrunched in the crowd
where millions gather daily
her Coptic cross hangs by her neck
a taxi swings toward the street's edge
hand reaches out the window
to rip the symbol of Egypt
from her neck.

Sixty Kph Prayer

Heading east out of Cairo's madness

priest behind the wheel

a man pulls beside

and yells:

Izkurnī fī ṣalawātak.

Remember me in your prayers.

The priest shouts back

Ismak eh?

What's your name . . .

Out the window the sand begins gathering.

In Passing

There is something inside
each of us
that scurries toward the past
in our bodies a rooted history
perhaps in the balls of our feet
a microscopic yearning
that floats inside that sphere
yearning in a language we've forgotten.

History is too in our knees
in the ball that pops
& twists as we journey.

And for those of us blessed to be old
& for those of us blessed to be young
it lives inside the tiny ball of skin
deep inside the belly button
tickles recollections from our tongues
stories of stories from then—

history lives in circles & spheres

floating

always suspended

waiting for release.

Al-Shi^cr Min Ghayr Ism

This is the way we conjure ourselves
break sound barriers
and tear down fences
in the valley of indecision.

                              This is the way
                 we shake dew from the drums
                           and beat rhythms of
                    jagged peaked symphonics.

This is how we communicate
to educate in the mire
of stagnation.

                              This is what we do
                           when we do what
                               we are . . .

Imagine being a manifestation
imagine becoming ancestry,
whole in lineage
and forever.

Al-Shi^cr Min Ghayr Ism is Arabic for "the poem with no name."

Living Ancients

For those of us young
healthy
we will face the mourning of our elders.
Bury them beneath
the earth.
And for those of us
who believe the living
ever-live
we will stand by the graves of our teachers
and know that we
like those we've buried
are living ancients.

Twenty-first Century Poem

And we became this way
through seasons of change
& radical shifts on the wind
through bloodied streets
& tough-labored births
technology & assimilation
have fed us all
something swinging
through constant struggle
& stiff-muscled survival
through spirit & verve
song & breath
we've made it
to this place of complacency
this place where things are
just as they were in the beginning

Remember Me

There are things
inside each one of us
that no one
but the night knows.
These are the things that make
everything possible.

The river of God is filled with water
and all I have is the hope to swim.

Where We Come From

semi-automatic machine fire
barreling through
freedom for hire

our homelands becoming
first world garbage dumps

too much internal posturing
not enough external interrogation

rising from cane fields & potted mint leaves
naˁnāˁ breath & cellophane feet

eating *rummān* & *tamr hind*
escaping into juice-glitter

> in places where the list of murdered
> surpasses the dead by natural causes

hunger is not the birthright of the children

retinas glare with coals of sandstone

muddied waters are the fertile of servile

in places where the list of murdered
surpasses the dead by natural causes

children dream of parrot fish in coral sunshine

dusty streets are filled with bright fabric
'cause weaving is the art of prayer

trash heaps rise like sky-water

doves fly over waves crying

in places where the list of murdered
surpasses the dead by natural causes

mirrors reflect lies

ʿafarīt lurk in crop soil

children learn from coal-burned corn

hieroglyphs speak truths

conquest sleeps in the neighbor's house

people hide colonial shoes under beds

44

someone walks on the dunes of ruin

we sing reality
through blue lotus songs

in places where the list of murdered
surpasses the dead by natural causes

politicians pay surgeons
to sew their eyes shut
& launch cannons in their ears

naʿnāʿ: Arabic; mint
rummān: Arabic; pomegranate
tamr hind: Arabic; tamarind
ʿafarīt: Arabic; evil spirits or ghosts, similar to the West Indian "duppy"

For Tātā

Time will tell, think you're in heaven
but you're living in hell.
—BOB MARLEY

Her spirit has departed
  It is here with me

Her spirit has departed
  It is here with me

The Zionists ravaged Bethlehem today
set fire to the Church of the Nativity

Judas sold out Jesus today
for thirty pieces of silver

My grandmother, she has reposed
Her spirit has departed

"From prophet even unto priest
everyone dealeth falsely"

Let her not deal with fault
may she rise beyond it
beyond this earth where the sacred is torched
where the false powers see no space for the Holy

Let her depart with a chariot & wings
bills cuffed inside her palms
alms for the poor

May she rejoice on reunion
with my *Giddū* whose love is dignified
by the crafts of his hands

May her children sing steady & our words
help guide her home

My *Tātā* who is the manifestation of love
selfless in her 8,000-mile journey
to be with her children and grandchildren
whose body now rests separate
from her rest
may you be united by waves
larger than the trans-Atlantic journey you took

You have returned home
to return home
your weary body has taken the journey
of this grandson's heart

May God rest you by the banks of our river.

The *hawa* of the Nile will forever be scented of you.

Spring

Make it to be sweet
like the hull of a ship breaking ocean's wake

Make it to be sweet
so we can see each other in reflection of our lips

Make it to be sweet
like the arch of the back at the touch of embrace

Make it to be sweet
like the beats of hip-hop when they speak to real

Make it to be sweet
so our hearts can sing the song of our feet

Make it to be sweet
so we can stay this way till the record's done

The Democratic National Convention

Los Angeles, August 18, 2000

People protest
police brutality
so the L.A.P.D.
beats the hell out of them
raining down midnight billy clubs
on the bilingual highway
where color means a beating
if your taillight flashes
anything other
than English.

Prelude to a Journey

The struggle is not in the wave
or the fury   but the silence of ocean's calm
the granules of sand separated
by omnipotent wind.

Be careful of the ripples in the bay
of the places where water kissed shore.

Be wary of lingering clouds
the shuttering voices of sky.

Understand that in the end
it is silence of heart that will kill us
the muffled song
that will cut off our feet.

A Poem for the Educational Institutions That Treat Us Raw

You pack 9 mm curriculum guns
& point them at our faces
shout confederate anthems of canonical chants
tsk tsk the way we
take your language & perfect its cadence
you rhyme money with success
& ask for tips
give positions to the stagnant
who take no risk
you share bread with the mongrels
& invite us to eat
pay attention and smile
when your "diversity" board meets
you approach us with ignorance
knowing we ain't you
& hope with good note-taking
we'll get it right

you equate color with posters
& close down educational borders
picketing with signs that read:

ANGLO SPOKEN HERE!

Enough

The blood of the dead is not negotiable!
—CHILEAN PROTESTERS IN OPPOSITION TO GENERAL PINOCHET

It's happening again

It never stopped

I am living in the war that each of my ancestors died for

I am living in the bomb marked "revenge" whose steel will
    burst on the necks of my brethren
whose toxins will leak into the water of my children's thirst

how many years must our children watch
the building of caskets, the withering of leaves
by graveside, by tombstone, by the rotting corpses
of their peers?

I am flying in the plane whose destruction can only be seen
    in infrared, whose image of humanity is a radar screen

we are a sharp-edged machine
moving for your table
the ax of my tongue is oiled
its muscles tense for striking

I am living in the rifle adorned with stickers from sixteen-
    year-old soldiers who pretend that this life is normal

our trees are fed by the blood of our sisters
our fruit is sour, our soil is rich
our children wail shards of glass
our youth wear guns for shoes

> I am an angry mob whose rage is fueled by falling stocks,
> who does not have time to care for the hungry, the
> disheveled, or the dead

hear my voice
my brother has ripped his heart from deep
beneath his ribs and left it on your plate
you have not seen freedom—the eyes
of the dead lurk inside your hollow skull

> I am living in the tent of Palestinian children who wake
> each morning to stand in the line marked "displacement,"
> who speak a language that is not enough

> > *the blood of the dead is not negotiable*
> > *the wine of the wicked not sweet*

> I am living in the land of a regime that calls itself a nation
> under God that shows no respect for creation

> > *the blood of the dead is not negotiable*
> > *the wine of the wicked not sweet*

> I am living in Babylon somewhere between New York and L.A.

> > *the blood of the dead is not negotiable*
> > *the wine of the wicked not sweet*

I am living in the repetition of hysteria, a misanthropic
record that spins over and over on a player so broke, no
one can stop it

the blood of the dead is not negotiable
the wine of the wicked not sweet

I am living in a lake of tears that knows no border, a place
where the salt is abundant and the rivers dry

the blood of the dead is not negotiable
the wine of the wicked not sweet

I am living in America in this place that has spit on every-
thing I know to love

Waiting

from the mouth of silence

comes trailing winds

shaping the elephant's tusk

Reclaiming the Classroom
(*after* Three for Phil McGee)

for John-Carlos Perea, colleague & composer
of the struggle; brother on bass

The drummer warms his song
by splitting a blade of grass.
Somewhere between dewdrops
and wet earth, the rhythm begins.

  Sing sweet friend, sing
Pay tribute in times of tore-up nations
on days when the sun spells
g i v e t h a n k s
and clouds remind us of those we've tried to forget.

John-Carlos you tell time in fret increments

bouncing into notions of remembrance
your bass songs, woven with liquid and flesh
like pomegranates split with broken glass
the "urban" Indian moving through city blocks
pulling mottoes from the sky
making music-memory

John-Carlos you wrote this one for our elders
educators of pavement wisdom, asphalt blues

wrote with verve
rote with verve

reclamation songs fluttering from
saxophone licks called back on a trip gone north

this is how it feels to remember
to remember the horizon before sunset
to understand that once we've gone, we've just begun
this journey, this first-dance, the dance
we bring to our classrooms
the dance you keep tucked at your nape
as an offering

and with your songs
your offerings
you gave me San Francisco
shaped it into something tangible
made the bridges my Nile
so I could give thanks again
and understand that brothers live near every river
and brothers sing in every voice
that in a time of rampant bombings
an offered song can bring us peace
or move us to something greater
that thing that's greater than peace
that prayer we call justice

to teach us to release
and catch ourselves again
syncopated pomegranates
flecked with marrow red

rejuvenation
rejoice
rejuvenation
we're taking this one back
we're gonna take this one back, way back,

back to the day when
yeah when yeah
when we could when we
could can can
like the colors of the toucan
we can dance

this first dance

just as dance

just as dance

justice dance

Fire Rhythms

for Jimmy Biala

Jimmy slams his hand on the cajón
                                  brings Cuba to the room

spreads his lips to smile
                        reverberates with elbow to the conga

I've seen you pounce and chime your way through space

open doors with kulintangs
                         and cast off demons
with flexitone words

Man, I've seen you move through time
                               like a tin can flailing
and set fire to a-go-go trees

Jimmy, your music's a peninsula
where water fills between crevices
                  & urchin rhythms climb the walls

your feet dig furrows for bass lines
& plant seeds for coming rain

Light it up on the down-beat brother
& fill that stage with smokes of sound

Find the road where the mountain curves
& sound it out

Shape the plantain into a cowbell
& ring that suckah till the sun come up!

Shouting Back the Place

I carry my name
     to the pinnacles
& redirect its ingenuity
     into folding spires
of unseen light
     shouting from corners of break-beat
drum solos
     my name goes echoing
down corridors of funk.
     Once, the rhythm of my name
reverberated so long
     it caught the windswept wave
of Mediterranea
     and rode that surge
all the way down to Aswân.
     Etched on the columns
of Horace's temple
     my name shouts
bird & eagle vision
     & still the crocodile swims the Nile
paddling in patterns of my name.

Al-Manṣūra (Nile Blues)

for my pops

In villages where wealth is food
my sisters cook for peace
and I lie sweating, wondering
where do I go from here?

In the city where my father was born
the Nile Delta
where blues squeaked out
of *'ūd* string treble
banks riffing to the dance
of smooth-flowing water

My father takes me back
to that place
where pains made way to a resister
to you
who made this man a man
in a time of warring nations

I take these words
from beneath the wings you gave me
and make them brave
to combat all our histories

Al-Manṣūra: Arabic; a city in the Nile Delta
'ūd: Arabic; a traditional short-necked Egyptian lute

For Charles Mingus & That Ever-Living "Love Chant"

after Quincy Troupe

pluckin from real to surreal, and back again
your bass line shifts roots, gnarling trees into singing children
resurrecting tired bones into swinging feet
all the while ringing the song of your Afro-Asian roots
taking us all on the ride & fall of deep-space swinging
like the floating verve of "Bird" and those before you
you can wrap it all up in the dark wood of your hollow bass
make it sing like the quieting love of eagles mating in flight
break-down note for note you've paved the streets of reverberating
cadence, Mingus moving thru space with that four-string bass
creating the nimbus of atmospheric jazz & raining down smooth streaks of
love, chanting like two-toned whirls swirling through water like ripples
of come-back-home blues, gyrating instrumental geese flying toward
reformatory refuge of wailing bass lines & smooth-feathered solos
you've got love, Charlie, chanting with your outstretched arms, moving
strings like a slide-by grooving, tracing knee to inner knee your lover rests
at the echoing space of every last note, calling across for something more

Survival

for Simon Ortiz

Strip it to bone
and watch it grow again.
Thrust a stick in the sand
and reap its fruits for wisdom.
When the bone grows whole
strip it again
and with exactness, shave it thin.
Punch a hole in the sliver
and wear it around your neck.
Remember your name
your marrow
and by whose blood you survive.

After the World Trade Center Is Destroyed, America Waves Its True Flag, the Crimson, Brown Men's Blood

for Adel Karas, murdered September 16, 2001

Air and water are the only consolations now
fire adulterated by the tip of a gun
we're down in the valley now
sayin' it was a robbery, they took no money,
shot him, called him dead in their ignorance
as if a gun could kill
down in the valley
there was a getaway car, and no money
just the laughter from speeding windows
they rid america of one more . . . or so they thought
my brother, our faces have been stolen
and we are dry like the soil that starves its children
withering the crops as they reach for sustenance

down in the valley

original of the nile
but in this place called america
we are all brown
unified by being objectified

I call now for rebellion
rebellion like the hand reaching for what it cannot hold
the child whose dignity is greater than her beating
to survive beyond the soil
to see beyond your self
believing only one

my brother who has left this world too soon
I will reclaim your face
from down in this valley
and bring it wrapped in myrrh
to your children who wear it well

Dispatches from the New World Order

Standing on solid earth
It is clear that we have lost something
In this space of forever crossings and collapsible borders
This space of translucent snaking and palm shadow adaptations

We used to have jobs, he says,
something to help sustain us,
something to reaffirm our humanity
through the ancient wisdom of work
now we have nothing but dissipating time
a horizon that reeks of death
we learn the steps for a coming bone dance
we are destined to be skeletons encircling ravines

How do you articulate
indigenous sense that rises from streets like mist?
How do you convey
the reality that land can speak culture's song?

We eclipse the moon with styrofoam
and ravage ourselves with jingle madness
articulating a corporate narrative
and suffocating the breath of story-speakers

we crawl through epithet forests
craving the singular answer
forgetting that our fallen brothers are the only soothsayers on this land
and their voices are anything but lonesome

Language

Incessant, pushing for the struggle
of re-generation
      one hurricane
replaces another
just when the island has been rejuvenated

Living in kaleidoscope cities
urban twisted metal sculptures
piles of moving fabric
& hair
all that hair, braided together
like a downtown skyline
woven through towers
with a one-two break-beat

Even these buildings have rhythm
metalworker songs
& saw blade scratches
      take them as a symbol
of our rise-up stance
educate our children for a second chance

Ain't no three strikes in the world I live in

We speak forgiveness
like giraffe tongues
long & ready to unravel

We speak change
in the language of the playground
the dialect of freeways and b-ball courts

We understand that nothing happens without a declaration
    even independence

So we declare this place our home
and push forward with those who push
& move past the ones whose feet can catch no rhythm
whose lives remain cemented in a history
unchanged   plagued by the parliament of greed

We declare an eastern expansion
a manifest where the west must rest
& leave its tired self behind

We speak ancestor codes of
handshake body language
& "brother I got your back"

We speak cross-generational tongues
of bilingual *I love you*s
& grand-parental recognition

We break things down to the critical
so that each generation can link to the next
    without severance

We speak in the grand tongue of humanity
a language without saliva
an underground dialect
whose code will be deciphered
and whose only script will read:

"Daughter, son, we're ready for you."

ACKNOWLEDGMENTS

"Dispatches from the New World Order" originally appeared in the *San Francisco Chronicle* and will be reprinted in *The Other Side of the Postcard*, edited by Devorah Major (City Lights Books, 2005).

"Where We Come From," "Al Manṣūra (Nile Blues)," and "After the World Trade Center Is Destroyed, America Waves Its True Flag, the Crimson, Brown Men's Blood" originally appeared in *Arab American and Diaspora Literature*; edited by Nathalie Handal (Interlink Books, 2005).

"A Prayer for My People" originally appeared in *Runes: A Review of Poetry.*

"Enough" originally appeared in *Poets Against the War;* edited by Sam Hamill (Nation Books, 2003).

"The Democratic National Convention" and "Remembering" originally appeared in *Antennae.*

"New Cairo" and "Transporting a Weed Whacker Way Over County Lines." originally appeared in *Prism.*

FUNDER ACKNOWLEDGMENTS

Coffee House Press is an independent nonprofit literary publisher. Our books are made possible through the generous support of grants and gifts from many foundations, corporate giving programs, individuals, and through state and federal support. This book received special project support from the Jerome Foundation in celebration of the Jerome Hill Centennial and in recognition of the valuable cultural contributions of artists to society. Coffee House Press receives general operating support from the Minnesota State Arts Board, through an appropriation by the Minnesota State Legislature and from the National Endowment for the Arts, a federal agency. Coffee House receives major funding from the McKnight Foundation, and from Target. Coffee House also receives significant support from: an anonymous donor; the Buuck Family Foundation; the Bush Foundation; the Patrick and Aimee Butler Family Foundation; Consortium Book Sales and Distribution; the Foundation for Contemporary Performance Arts; Stephen and Isabel Keating; the Lerner Family Foundation; the Outagamie Foundation; the Pacific Foundation; the law firm of Schwegman, Lundberg, Woessner & Kluth, P.A.; the James R. Thorpe Foundation; West Group; the Woessner Freeman Family Foundation; and many other generous individual donors.

This activity is made possible in part by a grant from the Minnesota State Arts Board, through an appropriation by the Minnesota State Legislature and a grant from the National Endowment for the Arts.

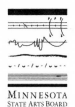

MINNESOTA
STATE ARTS BOARD

NATIONAL
ENDOWMENT
FOR THE ARTS

To you and our many readers across the country,
we send our thanks for your continuing support.

Good books are brewing at coffeehousepress.org

COLOPHON

Somewhere Else was designed at Coffee House Press
in the warehouse district of downtown Minneapolis.
The text is set in Caslon with Officina titles.